+ website

the Law of **fundraising**

2024 Supplement

Sixth Edition

BECOME A SUBSCRIBER!

Did you purchase this product from a bookstore?

If you did, it's important for you to become a subscriber. John Wiley & Sons, Inc. may publish, on a periodic basis, supplements and new editions to reflect the latest changes in the subject matter that you *need to know* in order to stay competitive in this ever-changing industry. By contacting the Wiley office nearest you, you'll receive any current update at no additional charge. In addition, you'll receive future updates and revised or related volumes on a 30-day examination review.

If you purchased this product directly from John Wiley & Sons, Inc., we have already recorded your subscription for this update service.

To become a subscriber, please call 1-877-762-2974 or send your name, company name (if applicable), address, and the title of the product to:

mailing address:	**Supplement Department** **John Wiley & Sons, Inc.** **10475 Crosspoint Blvd.** **Indianapolis, IN 46256**
e-mail:	**subscriber@wiley.com**
fax:	**1-800-605-2665**
online:	**www.wiley.com**

For customers outside the United States, please contact the Wiley office nearest you:

Professional & Reference Division
John Wiley & Sons Canada, Ltd.
90 Eglinton Ave. E. Suite 300
Toronto, Ontario M4P 2Y3
Canada
Phone: 416-236-4433
Phone: 1-800-567-4797
Fax: 416-236-8743
Email: canada@wlley.com

John Wiley & Sons Australia, Ltd.
42 McDougall Street
Milton, Queensland 4064
AUSTRALIA
Phone: 61-7-3859-9755
Fax: 61-7-3859-9715
Email: aus-custservice@wiley.com

John Wiley & Sons, Ltd.
European Distribution Centre
New Era Estate
Oldlands Way
Bognor Regis, West Sussex
PO22 9NQ, UK
Phone: (0)1243 779777
Fax: (0)1243 843 123
Email: customer@wlley.co.uk

John Wiley & Sons (Asia) Pte., Ltd.
1 Fusionopolis Walk
#07-01 Solaris South Tower
SINGAPORE 138628
Phone: 65-6302-9838
Fax: 65-6265-1782
Customer Service: 65-6302-9800
Email: asiacart@wiley.com

+ website

the Law of **fundraising**

2024 Supplement

Sixth Edition

Alicia M. Beck and
Bruce R. Hopkins

WILEY

Published by John Wiley & Sons, Inc., Hoboken, New Jersey.
Published simultaneously in Canada.

For general information on our other products and services or for technical support, please contact our Customer Care Department within the United States at (800) 762-2974, outside the United States at (317) 572-3993 or fax (317) 572-4002.

Wiley publishes in a variety of print and electronic formats and by print-on-demand. Some material included with standard print versions of this book may not be included in e-books or in print-on-demand. If this book refers to media such as a CD or DVD that is not included in the version you purchased, you may download this material at http://booksupport.wiley.com. For more information about Wiley products, visit www.wiley.com.

Library of Congress Cataloging-in-Publication Data:

ISBN 9781119873440 (Main Book)
ISBN 9781394244508 (Paperback)
ISBN 9781394244539 (ePDF)
ISBN 9781394244515 (ePub)

Cover image: © Comstock/Getty Images
Cover design: Wiley

SKY10069252_031124

Contents

Contents

A Letter to the Reader

It is with a heavy heart that we relay the news to you that Bruce Richard Hopkins, J.D., LL.M., S.J.D., passed away on October 31, 2021. Bruce's love for the law and for writing resulted in a wonderful relationship with Wiley that lasted for better than 30 years. Throughout that time, Bruce penned more than 50 books as well as writing "The Bruce R. Hopkins' Nonprofit Counsel" (a newsletter published monthly for 40 years). Bruce's texts are practical guides about nonprofits written for both lawyers AND for laypeople, many of which are considered vital to law libraries across the country. The ideas just kept flowing.

Beloved by many, Bruce was often referred to as the "Dean of Nonprofit Law." His teaching muscle was built over a period of 19 years when he was Professional Lecturer in Law at George Washington University National Law Center. As Professor from Practice at the University of Kansas, School of Law, Bruce exercised his generative spirit teaching and mentoring younger colleagues. Always the legal scholar, he could brilliantly take complicated concepts and distill them into easily understood principles for beginners, seasoned colleagues, and those unfamiliar with the subject matter. He was a presenter and featured speaker, both nationally and internationally, at numerous conferences throughout his career, among them Representing and Managing Tax-Exempt Organizations (Georgetown University Law Center, Washington, D.C.) and The Private Foundations Tax Seminar (El Pomar Foundation, Colorado Springs, Colorado). He practiced law in Washington, D.C., and Kansas City, Missouri, for over 50 years, receiving numerous awards and forms of recognition for his efforts

Bruce will be dearly missed, not solely for his contributions to the Wiley catalog, but because Bruce was a wonderful person who was dearly loved and respected both by all of us at Wiley and by all of those whom he encountered.

Preface

This 2024 supplement is the second supplement to accompany the sixth edition of this book. The supplement covers developments in the law of fundraising for charitable purposes as of the close of 2023.

I appreciate the assistance I have received from John Wiley & Sons in the preparation of this supplement. My thanks are extended, in particular, to my development editor, Brian T. Neill, and to Deborah Schindlar, managing editor, for their assistance and support in connection with this supplement.

Alicia M. Beck
March 2024

+ website

the Law of fundraising

2024 Supplement

Sixth Edition

CHAPTER ONE

Government Regulation of Fundraising for Charity

§ 1.2 CHARITABLE FUNDRAISING: A PORTRAIT

pp. 9–11. *Replace the text and headings with the following:*

(a) Scope of Charitable Giving in General

Charitable giving in the United States in 2022 is estimated to have totaled $ 499.33 billion.[25.1] Giving by individuals in 2022 amounted to an estimated $319.04 billion (declining 6.4% in 2022). Grantmaking by private foundations grew 2.5 percent to an estimated $105.21 billion in 2022. Giving by bequest totaled an estimated $45.60 billion in 2022, growing by 2.3 percent over 2021. Giving by corporations is estimated to have increased by 3.4 percent in 2022, totaling $29.48 billion (a decline of 4.2 percent, adjusted for inflation). Corporate giving includes cash and in-kind contributions made through corporate giving programs as well as grants and gifts made by corporate foundations.

Contributions to religious organizations in 2022 totaled $ 143.57 billion, the largest percentage of giving recipients in that year. Giving to human services reached $71.98 billion in 2022, and declined by 0.6% in current dollars, staying relatively flat with 2021. Giving to education is estimated to have declined -3.6 percent between 2021 and 2022 to $70.07 billion. Adjusted for inflation, giving to education organizations declined 10.7 percent. Giving to foundations is estimated to have increased by 10.1 percent in 2022 to $56.84 billion. Giving to health is estimated to have grown by 5.1 percent between 2021 and 2022 (a decline of 2.6 percent, adjusted for inflation) to $51.08 billion.

Giving to public-society benefit organizations decreased an estimated 8.4 percent between 2021 and 2022 to $46.86 billion. Giving to international affairs is estimated to be $33.71 billion in 2022, growing over 2021 with 10.9 percent growth. Giving to arts, culture, and humanities is estimated to have increased 2.9 percent between 2021 and 2022 to $24.67 billion. Giving to environmental and animal organizations is estimated to have decreased 1.6 percent between 2021 and 2022 to $16.10 billion.

(b) Online Charitable Fundraising

Not that many years ago, use of the Internet for charitable fundraising was only nascent. One analysis of online fundraising, in its beginnings, did not have statistics on this approach to gift solicitation.[25.1] But it was clearly coming, and was expected to someday be a major force in charitable fundraising. Now that "someday" has arrived.

In mid-2014, *The Chronicle of Philanthropy* gave a special report on online fundraising with the theme being "Digital Giving Goes Mainstream."[25.2] Among the findings in this report was that Internet gifts had climbed 13 percent in 2013 in relation to 2012, although online fundraising "still accounts for a very small portion of the money charities rely on."[25.3] Nonetheless, in 2013, the Leukemia & Lymphoma Society raised more than $98 million online, the California Community Foundation raised more than $95 million online, and the American Heart Association raised $59 million in that manner; other totals were more than $45 million (World Vision), about $40 million (Campus Crusade for Christ International, Cystic Fibrosis Foundation, National Christian Foundation, Salvation Army), about $30 million (March of Dimes Foundation, Young Life), and about $20 million (Global Impact, Memorial Sloan Kettering Cancer Center, United States Fund for Unicef, University of Michigan).[25.4]

About one year later, another report speaks of the "transformative promise of online fundraising" that has yet to materialize.[25.5] This report looks at the "short history of online fundraising" and finds that it "is not without signs of progress." It summarizes the successes of online-giving websites and notes that "[y]ear to year, more people give money online to charity." Still, for most charitable organizations, this report states that online giving

25.1. Hopkins, *The Nonprofits' Guide to Internet Communication Law* (John Wiley & Sons, 2003), Chapter 4.

25.2. 26 *Chron. of Phil.* (No. 13) F-1 (May 22, 2014).

25.3. Daniels and Narayanswamy, "Online Giving Grows More Sophisticated," 26 *Chron. of Phil.* (No. 13) F-3 (May 22, 2014).

25.4. 26 *Chron. of Phil.* (No. 13) F-4 (May 22, 2014).

25.5. "Click, Click, Cash?" 27 *Chron. of Phil.* (No. 9) 10 (May 2015).

"represents a sliver of their overall fundraising." The "promised revolution" is "moving at glacial speed" because of ancient tech infrastructure, reluctance on the part of fundraising management to place more emphasis on online operations, and lack of understanding by senior executives and board members of the potential of online fundraising. This report concludes that "effective online fundraising doesn't eliminate the human touch at the core of giving." Every day, the report states, "you see more meaning and substance on the Internet, more people forging thoughtful, deep connections—deeper connections, perhaps than a professional fundraiser could ever hope for with a yearly newsletter."[25.6]

p. 12. *Delete the text preceding the heading.*

§ 1.3 EVOLUTION OF GOVERNMENT REGULATION OF FUNDRAISING

p. 15. *Insert the following after the first full paragraph of text:*

On February 18, 2022, New York Attorney General Letitia James filed a civil complaint against Shirley Goddard, the former executive director and chair of the board of directors of the Humanitarian Organization for Multicultural Experiences, Inc. (H.O.M.E.) and her husband Tyrone Goddard. It is alleged that between 2012 and 2018, Mrs. Goddard improperly diverted or misused nearly a million dollars in H.O.M.E.'s charitable assets for her personal gain. Mr. Goddard, the former board chair, was aware of and helped to conceal his wife's unlawful conduct. The money that the Goddards stole hindered H.O.M.E.'s ability to fulfill its mission to provide critical services to individuals with developmental disabilities in the Syracuse area. The attorney general's complaint seeks restitution of the funds that were diverted from H.O.M.E. as well as a permanent bar on any fiduciary role for Shirley or Tyrone Goddard in any New York charitable organization.

State charity officials continue to crack down on charities engaging in unauthorized and unethical activities. The following examples are taken from the National Association of State Charity Officials (NASCO)'s Annual Report on State Enforcement and Regulation.

On January 26, 2021, the FTC, 38 states, and the District of Columbia filed a multistate action against Michigan-based professional fundraiser Associated Community Services (ACS), two businesses related to ACS, and the owners/operators of each of those businesses (the "ACS defendants"). Other defendants

25.6. *Id.* at 11, 12, 14, 16, 19. In general, "The Best of Online Fundraising," articles beginning on pp. 9, 10, 12, 14, 16, 18, 20, and 22, 28 *Chron. of Phil.* (No. 7) (May 2016).

included Directele and The Dale Corporation and their owners and managers (the "Directele defendants") that operated as ACS spin-off fundraising companies. The ACS defendants and Directele defendants made billions of solicitation calls nationally on behalf of multiple charities almost exclusively using soundboard technology (robocalls). Callers used deceptive claims about the charities, and collected more than $110 million, almost all of which went to the defendants, not to charitable programs. Under the court-ordered settlements, the defendants are subject to a $110-million judgment, which was partially suspended. Funds collected were distributed via cy pres to three not-for-profit corporations. Also, under the settlement, all defendants were permanently prohibited from engaging in charitable fundraising.[42.1]

On January 12, 2021, the states of California, Florida, Illinois, Maryland, Minnesota, New Mexico, Ohio, Oregon, Washington, and the Commonwealth of Virginia announced a settlement agreement with the Healing Heroes Network, a veterans' charity based in Florida. The states found that the organization had falsely promised to use donations to help wounded veterans of the wars in Iraq and Afghanistan receive medical treatments that the Department of Veterans Affairs did not readily provide. The charity also falsely claimed on social media in 2016 and 2017 to dedicate 100 percent of proceeds to wounded veterans. The investigation revealed that very little of the contributions received by the Healing Heroes Network, Inc., were used to further this charitable mission. Under the settlement agreement, the defendants agreed to permanently cease all charitable solicitations, and the individual defendants will pay $95,000 to the State of Washington to be used by a veterans' charity whose mission matches the representations made by Healing Heroes Network. The individual defendants are also banned from overseeing, managing, or soliciting charitable contributions for any nonprofit organization for five years.[42.3]

On May 24, 2021, the Kansas Office of the Attorney General secured a judgment against A Ride for the Wounded. A Ride for the Wounded and its owner were permanently banned from doing business in Kansas and ordered to pay more than $11,000 in damages that were used for personal expenses in violation of the Kansas Charitable Organizations and Solicitations Act. In May 2021, the Maryland Attorney General's Office entered into an assurance of voluntary compliance (AVC) with the Animal Welfare Society of Howard County. The AVC followed a cease and desist order that had been issued in

42.1. See https://www.ftc.gov/legal-library/browse/cases-proceedings/162-3208-associated-community-services-inc.

42.3. See https://www.marylandattorneygeneral.gov/press/2021/011221.pdf.

August 2019. The Maryland OAG alleged that the organization had made false and misleading solicitations, willfully submitted materially false registration information, and made a misrepresentation that was likely to affect a person's decision to make a contribution. The organization underwent internal changes and installed new leadership. New leadership was able to satisfy the issue addressed in the cease and desist order. The AVC allows the organization to solicit in Maryland again and levies a $15,000 penalty. The penalty will be waived if the organization complies with all provisions of the assurance of voluntary compliance. And on July 23, 2021, the Michigan Attorney General and the Michigan Department of Licensing and Regulatory Affairs obtained a default judgment dissolving 10 fraudulent entities for failing to comply with state nonprofit and charity laws and permanently enjoining defendants from serving as an officer or director of a Michigan nonprofit or seeking a certificate of authority to operate a foreign nonprofit entity in the state. In 2020, the Department of the Attorney General identified defendants Ian Richard Hosang, Claudia Stephen, and Lincoln Palsey as involved with the fraudulent entities American Cancer Foundation (ACF) of Detroit, ACF of Grand Rapids, ACF of Lansing, and ACF of Michigan; American Cancer Society (ACS) of Detroit and ACS of Michigan; American Red Cross (ARC) of Detroit and ARC of Michigan; United Way of Detroit and United Way of Michigan.

In the area of executive compensation, on August 26, 2021, Attorney General Ashley Moody and Governor Ron DeSantis announced a global settlement agreement with Florida Coalition Against Domestic Violence (FCADV) and the organization's former CEO, Tiffany Carr. A complaint had been filed in March 2020, alleging that the FCADV board severely mismanaged funds, and that Ms. Carr had been paying herself excessive compensation. The settlement agreement requires former FCADV officers and directors to pay more than $3.9 million to Department of Children and Families (DCF) and the court-appointed receiver, including a more than $2 million payment by Ms. Carr. Per the settlement agreement, former FCADV officers Patricia Duarte and Sandra Barnett must pay a total of $60,000. FCADV insurers may pay the remaining funds from the $3.9 million payment, totaling more than $1.7 million. Additionally, more than $1 million currently in accounts of the FCADV's foundation will go directly to domestic violence centers across the state. The dissolution of FCADV will include a claims process for creditors, overseen by the receiver and court. The process will establish a claims priority, giving DCF priority as a creditor with an allowed claim of more than $2.8 million. There is a possibility of additional recovery by DCF through the liquidation of FCADV's assets, and the sale of property will be applied to the judgment balance. Additionally, FCADV will stipulate to a judgment for more than $6 million, with the $3.9 million settlement funds to be applied to the judgment balance. Under the settlement agreement, eight non-party state agencies agreed to provide releases to the directors and officers to facilitate the agreement.[42.4]

§ 1.4 CONTEMPORARY REGULATORY CLIMATE

p. 22. ***Insert the following immediately following the heading:***

In its 2021 Annual Report, the National Association of State Charity Officials listed the following as the four top trends and issues currently facing nonprofits: (1) it is a transitional time for many nonprofit and tax-exempt organizations, with financial strains and staff turnover; (2) increases in requests to borrow from restricted endowments and cy pres applications; (3) increases in online donations, "virtual" organizations, and viral charitable causes; and (4) lack of or delinquent charitable solicitation registrations.

42.4. See http://www.myfloridalegal.com/newsrel.nsf/newsreleases/35B3BC44ABBD0C38 8525873D00535E93?Open&.

CHAPTER FOUR

State Regulation of Fundraising

§ 4.16 CALIFORNIA LAW REGULATING CHARITABLE FUNDRAISING PLATFORMS

p. 223. *Insert replacing the final paragraph:*

On November 21, 2022, the California Department of Justice published a notice delaying implementation of these fundraising regulations, signaling the need for additional time to revise regulations in response to public comments received on the initial notice of proposed rulemaking issued earlier this year.

Overall, the text of the modified proposed regulations proposes substantial revisions to the initial proposal. Notable changes include amendments to the definitions of the types of charitable fundraising platforms that will be regulated, the time frame for remitting donated funds to recipient charitable organizations, and the information required to be provided to recipient charitable organizations with the donated funds. As of the end of 2022, the California DOJ had proposed delaying the effective date of the regulations to January 1, 2024 (although the operative provisions of AB 488 are set to take effect on January 1, 2023). The modified regulations do not explicitly state that the Department will refrain from enforcing compliance with the law in this interim period before final regulations are issued.

§ 4.17 KANSAS LAW

Insert following 4.16:

Protecting donor intent is essential for a culture of trust and accountability in the world of philanthropy. Donors should be able to give freely, knowing their intentions will be respected. Charities, in turn, must uphold the trust placed in them by honoring this donor intent and using donated funds in accordance with instructions. In April 2023, Kansas Governor Laura Kelly signed the landmark Donor Intent Protection Act[4.1] into law. This new statute, effective July 1, 2023, purports to make it easier for donors to enforce gift restrictions. It provides a legal pathway for the enforcement of written endowment agreements. The intent behind the Act was to encourage charitable giving by benefiting donors, charities, and the numerous individuals served by nonprofit organizations in Kansas.

This legislation protects the intent of Kansas donors and gives them the assurance their gifts will be used as they intended, while also providing a way to correct course in case of violations. In the past, donor intent has been violated by unfortunate instances resulting in complicated legal battles.

In 2016, Westminster College in Fulton, Missouri, violated donors' intent for grants when it tried to get $12.6 million from an endowment to fund its general operating budget. The president of the college had already withdrawn funds and was asking for more money to repay what was already spent without approval.[4.2] Another example is the case of The Ohio State University (OSU). A donor donated $30.3 million to OSU in 2001 to establish a permanent endowment supporting law school scholarships. It was later discovered that the endowment held less than the agreed-upon amount, and the number of scholarships provided was significantly less than what was originally intended, resulting in law graduates having to pay full price for their education. These examples illustrate how a breakdown of trust between donors and charities can have far-reaching impacts. Donors must have confidence their gifts will be used the way they intended.

Here are the operative sections of the Act:

> *Sec. 3. (a) Except where specifically required or authorized by federal or state law, including, but not limited to, K.S.A. 58-3616, and amendments thereto, no charitable organization that accepts a contribution of property of an endowment fund or to an endowment fund pursuant to an endowment agreement that imposes a written donor-imposed restriction shall violate the terms of that restriction.*
>
> *(b) If a charitable organization violates a donor-imposed restriction contained in an endowment agreement, the donor, or the donor's legal representative, may file a complaint within two years after discovery of the violation for breach of such agreement but not more than 40 years after the date of the endowment agreement that established the endowment fund. The complaint may be filed in a court of general jurisdiction in the county of this state where a charitable organization named as a party has its principal office or principal place of carrying out its*

4.1. S Sub for HB 2170.

4.2. In the end, Westminster was subjected to annual independent audit statements to the state attorney general's office.

charitable purpose or in the county of residence of the donor. The complaint may be filed whether or not the endowment agreement expressly reserves a right to sue or a right of enforcement. A complaint filed pursuant to sections 1 through 4, and amendments thereto, shall not seek, or result in, a judgment awarding damages to the plaintiff.

(c)(1) If the court determines that a charitable organization violated a donor-imposed restriction, the court may order any remedy in law or equity that is consistent with and restores, to the extent possible, the donor's intent as expressed by the donor-imposed restrictions and conditions in the endowment agreement, including, but not limited to:

(A) Future compliance with or performance of donor-imposed restrictions or conditions on the use or expenditure of the gifted endowment property;

(B) restitution or restoration by the charitable organization of property to an endowment fund that has been expended or used by the charitable organization in contravention of donor-imposed restrictions;

(C) an accounting or the imposition of accounting requirements;

(D) restoration or a change to a name required by the donor imposedrestrictions;

(E) measures to preserve the property and value of the endowment fund;

(F) modification or release of a donor-imposed restriction or reformation or dissolution of the endowment agreement as permitted by Kansas law; or

(G) transfer of property from the endowment fund to another charitable organization as directed by the donor, but only if the transfer would not jeopardize or be inconsistent with the tax-exempt status of the original charitable organization.

Nothing in this section shall conflict with or affect section 3(b), and amendments thereto.

(2) The court shall not order the return of donated funds to the donor or the donor's legal representative or estate.

Sec. 4. A charitable organization may obtain a judicial declaration of rights and duties expressed in an endowment agreement containing donor-imposed restrictions as to all of the actions that such agreement contemplates, including, but not limited to, the interpretation, performance and enforcement of the agreement and determination of its validity as provided in K.S.A. 58-3616, and amendments thereto. The charitable organization may also seek such declaration in any suit brought under this section.

. . . .

Nothing in this act affects the authority of the attorney general to enforce any restriction in an endowment agreement, limits the application of the judicial power of cy pres or alters the right of an institution to modify a restriction on the management, investment, purpose or use of an endowment fund in a manner permitted by the endowment agreement.

Attorney General Shuts Down Fraudulent Kansas Charities Former Kansas Attorney General Derek Schmidt banned defendants William Storms III and Kansas City FOP #1, his fraudulent charity, from doing business and operating as a charity in Kansas. The defendants were also required to turn over $10,000 they illegally raised to legitimate charitable organization the Bonner Springs Fraternal Order of Police Lodge No. 65. Investigators from the Attorney General's office's Consumer Protection Division found that Storms operated an unregistered charity and solicited donations for alleged charitable purposes. Similarly, Attorney General Schmidt found a Georgia man and his Kansas charity, A Ride for the Wounded, Inc., banned from doing business in Kansas and ordered to pay more than $11,000 in damages for violating the Kansas Charitable Organizations and Solicitations Act. Schmidt issued the following advice for Kansans making charitable contributions to keep these tips in mind:[4.3]

- **Support local, established charities**. While there are many large, international organizations that do great work, your donations can often have a greater impact when they support a cause close to your community, where you can see the results of your donations.
- **Watch out for names that sound alike**. Scammers often make their organizations' names sound very similar to other well-known charities.
- **Be careful with telemarketers requesting contributions**. Oftentimes, the telemarketer keeps a substantial portion of the donation. If you have questions about a solicitation, don't be afraid to reach out to the charity directly.
- **Ask questions to find out where your donations go**. Ask for written information, including how much of the money raised is actually used for charitable purposes and how much will end up in the hands of the professional fundraiser.
- **Ask if your donation is tax deductible**. Not all donations to charities are tax deductible. You can check a charity's status with the IRS at www.irs.gov. When in doubt, double-check with your tax preparer before assuming a donation will be tax deductible.
- **Document your donation**. Make the donation by credit card or check—not cash, wire transfer, or gift card. A solicitor who asks for payment by wire transfer or gift card is a red flag for scams. If something doesn't feel right to you, consider donating to a different cause. If you pay by check, make the check payable directly to the charitable organization, not to the fundraiser soliciting the donation. Ask for a receipt to show the amount of the donation and if you specified your donation toward a specific project.

4.3. *See* https://www.nasconet.org/tag/attorney-general-derek-schmidt/.

CHAPTER SIX

Federal Regulation of Fundraising

§ 6.16 CHARITABLE FUNDRAISING ORGANIZATIONS

(c) Other Exemption Issues

In IRS Letter 202305012, the IRS's rationale for revocation of Section 501(c)(3) status was that "the Organization's activities related to preparing for and assisting with the fundraising events of other entities [for a fee] demonstrate characteristics of a commercial business that doesn't further the Organization's tax-exempt purpose of education." Specifically:

> *While the Examiner agrees that the Organization provides training and education to other tax-exempt organizations, and that IRC Sec. 501(c)(3) and the Regulations thereunder do not preclude an organization that receives tax exemption for the purpose of education under this Code section from being able to specify the type and purpose of the education it provides, the examination clearly determined that the training and education the Organization provides is merely a means to the end of providing for-profit fundraising for other tax-exempt entities. Although there isn't necessarily anything wrong with providing these products and services to other tax-exempt organizations and doing so provides a great service to increase the fundraising efforts of these other tax-exempt organizations, the manner in which the Organization provides these products and services, along with the way the Organization handles all of the related financial transactions, is indicative of a commercial enterprise and not a tax-exempt purpose.*

Inflation-Adjusted Insubstantiality Threshold— $50 Test

Year	Amount	Rev. Proc.
1993	$62	92–102
1994	64	93–49
1995	66	94–72
1996	67	95–53
1997	69	96–59
1998	71	97–57
1999	72	98–61
2000	74	99–42
2001	76	2001–13
2002	79	2001–59
2003	80	2002–70
2004	82	2003–85
2005	83	2004–71
2006	86	2005–70
2007	89	2006–53
2008	91	2007–66
2009	95	2008–66
2010	96	2009–50
2011	97	2010–40
2012	99	2011–52
2013	102	2012–41
2014	104	2013–35
2015	105	2014–61
2016	106	2015–53
2017	107	2016–55
2018	108	2018–18
2019	111	2018–57
2020	112	2019–44
2021	113	2020–45
2022	117	2021–45
2023	125	2022–38
2024	132	2023–34

Inflation-Adjusted Insubstantiality Threshold— $25 Test

Year	Amount	Rev. Proc.
1990	$27.26	90–12
1991	28.58	92–58
1992	30.09	92–58
1993	31	92–102
1994	32	93–49
1995	33	94–72
1996	33.50	95–53
1997	34.50	96–59
1998	35.50	97–57
1999	36	98–61
2000	37	99–42
2001	38	2001–13
2002	39.50	2001–59
2003	40	2002–70
2004	41	2003–85
2005	41.50	2004–71
2006	43	2005–70
2007	44.50	2006–53
2008	45.50	2007–66
2009	47.50	2008–66
2010	48	2009–50
2011	48.50	2010–40
2012	49.50	2011–52
2013	51	2012–41
2014	52	2013–35
2015	52.50	2014–61
2016	53	2015–53
2017	53.50	2016–55
2018	54	2018–18
2019	55.50	2018–57
2020	56	2019–44
2021	56.50	2020–45
2022	58.50	2021–45
2023	62.50	2022–38
2024	66.00	2023–34

Inflation–Adjusted Low–Cost Article Definition

Year	Amount	Rev. Proc.
1990	$5.45	90–12
1991	5.71	92–58
1992	6.01	92–58
1993	6.20	92–102
1994	6.40	93–49
1995	6.60	94–72
1996	6.70	95–53
1997	6.90	96–59
1998	7.10	97–57
1999	7.20	98–61
2000	7.40	99–42
2001	7.60	2001–13
2002	7.90	2001–59
2003	8.00	2008–70
2004	8.20	2003–85
2005	8.30	2004–71
2006	8.60	2005–70
2007	8.90	2006–53
2008	9.10	2007–66
2009	9.50	2008–66
2010	9.60	2009–50
2011	9.70	2010–40
2012	9.90	2011–52
2013	10.20	2012–41
2014	10.40	2013–35
2015	10.50	2014–61
2016	10.60	2015–53
2017	10.70	2016–55
2018	10.80	2018–18
2019	11.10	2018–57
2020	11.20	2019–44
2021	11.30	2020–45
2022	11.70	2021–45
2023	12.50	2022–38
2024	13.20	2023–34

Table of Cases

Table of IRS Pronouncements

Revenue Rulings	Sections
54–243	6.7(b)
55–676	5.8(a)
56–152	5.8(a)
56–304	6.1
56–511	5.8(a)
59–330	5.8(b)
64–182	5.1(c), 5.9(b), 6.6, 6.16(b)
66–221	5.8(a)
67–4	5.9(b)
67–149	6.16(a)
67–246	5.1(a), 5.2
67–325	6.5
67–367	6.1
68–432	5.4(d)
69–268	5.75.8(a)
69–545	2.1
69–574	5.8(a)
69–633	5.8(a)
71–477	6.5
71–581	5.8(a), 5.8(b)
72–431	5.8(b)
73–504	6.3
75–201	5.8(b)
75–472	5.8(a)
76–204	2.1
77–72	5.8(b)
78–84	2.1
78–85	2.1
78–144	5.8(a)
80–108	6.2
80–200	2.1
80–286	2.1
81–178	5.8(a)
84–132	6.7(a)
85–184	6.7(b)
89–51	10.8(b)
92–49	5.2
98–15	6.6
2004–6	6.15(a)

Private Letter Rulings	Sections
7946001	5.8(b)
8127019	5.8(b)
8203134	5.8(b)
8232011	5.8(b)
8725056	5.8(b)
8747066	5.8(b)
8823109	5.8(b)
8832003	5.2
9250001	5.8(b)
9315001	5.6
9320042	5.8(a)
9450028	5.8(b)
9623035	5.4(a)
9703025	5.8(b)
9709029	5.8(b)
9712001	5.8(b)
9740032	5.8(a)
9810030	5.8(b)
9816027	5.8(b)
200022056	5.8(b)
200108045	5.8(b)
200114040	6.6
200128059	5.8(b)
200303062	6.8(b)
200443045	10.12(d)
200533001	6.7(k)
200634046	5.9(c)
200722028	5.8(b)
201103057	6.16(b)
201245025	6.16(c)
201251019	5.8(b)
201309016	6.16(c)
201310046	6.16(c)
201323037	6.17(c)
201332015	6.17(b)
201338052	6.1
201350042	6.16(c)
201407014	6.16(c)
201410035	6.16(c)

TABLE OF IRS PRONOUNCEMENTS

Private Letter Rulings	Sections
201415003	6.16(b)
201416010	6.16(c)
201429027	6.16(c)
201440023	6.16(c)
201442066	6.17(c)
201452017	6.16(c)
201503016	6.16(c)
201507026	6.16(c)
201517014	6.1
201523022	6.16(c)
201541013	5.7(a)
201544025	5.8(a)
201603039	5.9(c)
201630016	5.8(b)
201632022	6.16(b)
201635006	5.8(b)
201734009	5.8(b)
201814009	6.16(c)
201825032	5.8(b)
201843011	6.1
201847010	6.16(b)
202001023	5.7(b)
202127041	6.16(a)

Technical Advice Memoranda	Sections
9147007	5.8(b), 6.8(b)
9502009	5.8(b)
9509002	5.8(b)
9652004	5.8(b)
9712001	5.8(b)
9723001	5.8(b)
200021056	5.8(a)
200243057	5.7(a), 5.7(b), 5.12(f)
200244028	5.7(b)
200437040	5.7(a)
201544025	5.8(b), 6.17(a)
201633032	5.8(b)

Revenue Procedures	Sections
72–54	6.5
75–50	6.5
82–23	5.6
83–23	5.9
90–12	5.2
90–27	5.8
92–49	5.2
92–102	5.2
2019–22	6.5
2022–5	6.2(b)

Table of Cases Discussed in *Bruce R. Hopkins' Nonprofit Counsel*

The following cases, referenced in the text, are discussed in greater detail in one or more issues of the coauthor's monthly newsletter, as indicated.

Case	Book Sections	Newsletter Issues
Addis v. Commissioner	5.3	September 2002, September 2004, April 2005
Alumni Association of the University of Oregon, Inc. v. Commissioner	5.7	December 1999
American Bar Endowment v. United States	5.7, 5.4	April 1984, July 1985
American Campaign Academy v. Commissioner	5.13, 5.15	July 1989, June 2001
Americans for Prosperity v. Grewal	6.11(d), 8.12A	December 2019
Americans for Prosperity Foundation v. Becerra	6.11(d), 8.12A	November 2018
Americans for Prosperity Foundation v. Harris	6.11(d), 8.12A	March 2016, July 2016, August 2016
American Target Advertising v. Giani	4.2A, 4.3	November 1998, March 2000
Auburn Police Union v. Tierney	4.3	July 1991
Averyt v. Commissioner	5.3(c)	September 2012, May 2016
Bellotti v. Telco Communications, Inc.	4.3	May 1987
Big River Development, LLC v. Commissioner	5.3(c)	October 2017
Bob Jones University v. United States	2.1, 5.12	July 1985
Boone Operations Co., LLC v. Commissioner	5.3(c)	June 2013
Brentwood Academy v. Tennessee Secondary School Athletic Association	9.3	April 2001
Bullock et al. v. IRS	6.11(d)	October 2019, November 2019
Camps Newfound/Owatonna, Inc. v. Town of Harrison, Maine	4.2	July 1997
Capital Gymnastics Booster Club, Inc. v. Commissioner	5.26(c)(i)	November 2013
Caracci v. Commissioner	5.6	July 2002
Center for Competitive Politics v. Harris	6.11(d), 8.12A	July 2015, January 2016, January 2018
Church by Mail v. Commissioner	5.13	September 1985, December 1985, June 2001
Citizens Union of the City of New York v. Attorney General of State of New York	6.11(d)	December 2019
Citizens United v. Schneiderman	6.11(d)	October 2015, April 2018
College of the Desert Alumni Association, Inc. v. Commissioner	5.7(b)(iv)	April 2017
Common Cause v. Commissioner	5.7	August 1999
DiDonato v. Commissioner	5.3(c)	September 2011

(continued)

TABLE OF CASES DISCUSSED IN BRUCE R. HOPKINS' NONPROFIT COUNSEL

Case	Book Sections	Newsletter Issues
Disabled American Veterans v. Commissioner	5.7	April 1990
est of Hawaii v. Commissioner	5.13	June 2001
Executive Network Club, Inc. v. Commissioner	5.7	March 1995
Federal Trade Commission v. Mainstream Marketing Services, Inc.	5.21	December 2003
French v. Commissioner	5.3(c)	May 2016
Fund for the Study of Economic Growth and Tax Reform v. Internal Revenue Service	8.12	May 1998, February 1999
Giving Hearts, Inc. v. Commissioner	8.4(e)	October 2019
Hernandez v. Commissioner	3.2, 4.1, 4.7, 5.14	July 1989
Illinois v. Telemarketing Associates, Inc.	4.3(g)(vii), 8.11	December 2003
International Society for Krishna Consciousness v. Lee	4.3	May 1991, August 1992
Irby v. Commissioner	5.3(c)	December 2012
Jimmy Swaggart Ministries v. California Board of Equalization	4.3, 4.7	March 1990
Kentucky Bar Foundation, Inc. v. Commissioner	2.1	March 1985
Laborers' International Union of North America v. Commissioner	5.7	October 2001
Lintzenich v. United States	5.6(b)(viii)	December 2005
Losantiville Country Club v. Commissioner	5.7(a)(iii)	June 2017, October 2017
Mainstream Marketing Services, Inc. v. Federal Trade Commission	5.19	December 2003
McGrady v. Commissioner	8.12(d)	March 2017
National Collegiate Athletic Association v. Commissioner	5.7	April 1989, November 1990
National Foundation, Inc. v. United States	5.13	January 1998
National Water Well Association v. Commissioner	5.7	March 1989
Oregon State University Alumni Association, Inc. v. Commissioner	5.7	December 1999
Redlands Surgical Services v. Commissioner	5.13	September 1999, June 2001
Riley v. National Federation of the Blind of North Carolina	2.6, 4.3, 8.1	September 1998
RP Golf, LLC v. Commissioner	5.3(c)	December 2012, May 2016, July 2016, August 2017, September 2017
Rutkoske v. Commissioner	5.14(d)	October 2017
Ryan v. Telemarketing Associates, Inc.	4.3, 8.11	January 2003
Schrimsher v. Commissioner	5.3(c)	May 2011, May 2016
Secretary of State of Maryland v. Joseph H. Munson Co., Inc.	4.3, 4.4, 8.1	August 1984, January 1985, March 1985, July 1985
Senior Citizens of Missouri, Inc. v. Commissioner	5.13	March 1989
Sierra Club, Inc. v. Commissioner	5.7	July 1993, October 1994, August 1996, May 1999

TABLE OF CASES DISCUSSED IN BRUCE R. HOPKINS' NONPROFIT COUNSEL

Case	Book Sections	Newsletter Issues
Simmons v. Commissioner	5.3(c)	November 2009, May 2016
310 Retail, LLC v. Commissioner	5.3(c)	October 2017
Thomas More Law Center v. Becerra	6.11(d), 8.12A	November 2018
United Cancer Council v. Commissioner	5.6	January 1998, April 1999
United States v. American Bar Endowment	3.2, 5.1, 5.7	August 1986
United States v. NorCal Tea Party Patriots	5.15(d)	May 2016
U.S. Security v. Federal Trade Commission	5.21	December 2003
Veterans of Foreign Wars, Department of Michigan v. Commissioner	5.2, 5.7	August 1987
Veterans of Foreign Wars of the United States v. Department of Missouri, Inc.	5.2, 5.7	December 1984
Vigilant Hose Company of Emmitsburg v. United States	5.7	August 2001
Village of Schaumburg v. Citizens for a Better Environment	2.6, 4.2, 4.3, 9.1	January 1985, March 1985, July 1985
Watchtower Bible Tract Society of New York v. Village of Stratton	4.3	April 2002
Wendy L. Parker Rehabilitation Foundation, Inc. v. Commissioner	3.2	November 1986
West 17th Street LLC v. Commissioner	5.3(b)	
West 17th Street LLC v. Commissioner	5.3(b)	March 2017
WRG Enterprises, Inc. v. Crowell	4.3	February 1989
Zagfly v. Commissioner	5.26	April 2013, July 2015

Table of Private Letter Rulings and Technical Advice Memoranda Discussed in *Bruce R. Hopkins' Nonprofit Counsel*

The following IRS private letter rulings and technical advice memoranda, referenced in the text, are discussed in greater detail in one or more issues of the coauthor's monthly newsletter, as indicated.

PLR/TAM	Book Section	Newsletter Issue
9502009	5.7	February 1995
9712001	5.7	June 1997
9740032	5.7	December 1997
200114040	5.13	June 2001
200128059	5.7	September 2001
200230005	7.13	October 2002
200243057, 200437040	5.6, 5.6(a)(xii)	December 2002, November 2004
200533001	5.14(l)	November 2005
201103057	5.26(b)	March 2011
201245025	5.26(c)	January 2012
201251019	5.7(b)(ii)	March 2013
201309016	5.26, 5.26(c)	May 2013
201310046	5.26, 5.26(c)	May 2013
201323037	5.26(c)	August 2013
201332015	5.15(d), 5.26(b)	October 2013
201350042	5.26(c)	February 2014
201407014	5.26(c)	May 2014
201410035	5.26(c)	May 2014
201415003	5.26(b)	February 2014
201416010	5.26(c)	June 2014
201429027	5.26(c)	October 2014
201440023	5.26(c)	October 2014
201442066	20.11(b)	December 2014
201452017	4.10, 20.11	March 2015
201503016	4.10	March 2015
201507023	5.26(c)	April 2015
201523022	5.26(c)	August 2015
201541013	5.6(a)	December 2015
201544025	5.7(a)(i), 5.7(b)(iv), 5.26(a)	December 2015, January 2016
201630016	5.5(b)(i)	October 2016
201632022	5.26(c)(iii)	October 2016
201635006	5.7(b)(viii)	November 2016
201719004	8.12(d)	July 2017, August 2017
201734009	5.7(b)(vi-1)	November 2017
201814009	5.26(c)	June 2008

(*continued*)

PLR/TAM	Book Section	Newsletter Issue
201825032	5.7(b)	August 2018
202001018	5.15(c)	March 2020
202001023	5.6(b)(iii-a)	March 2020

Online Resources

The Law of Fundraising, Sixth Edition, 2024 Supplement is complemented by seven online resources. Please visit www.wiley.com/go/hopkins/lawoffundraising6e-2024supp to download the following tables in PDF format.

Appendices

- Inflation-Adjusted Insubstantiality Threshold—$50 Test
- Inflation-Adjusted Insubstantiality Threshold—$25 Test
- Inflation-Adjusted Low-Cost Article Definition

Tables

- Table of Cases
- Table of IRS Pronouncements
- Table of Private Letter Rulings and Technical Advice Memoranda Discussed in *Bruce R. Hopkins' Nonprofit Counsel*
- Table of Cases Discussed in *Bruce R. Hopkins' Nonprofit Counsel*

About the Authors

Bruce R. Hopkins was the principal in the Bruce R. Hopkins Law Firm, LLC, Kansas City, Missouri. He concentrated his practice on the representation of tax-exempt organizations. His practice ranged over the entirety of law matters involving exempt organizations, with emphasis on the formation of nonprofit organizations, acquisition of recognition of tax-exempt status for them, the private inurement and private benefit doctrines, governance, the intermediate sanctions rules, legislative and political campaign activities issues, public charity and private foundation rules, unrelated business planning, use of exempt and for-profit subsidiaries, joint venture planning, tax shelter involvement, review of annual information returns, the law of charitable giving, and fundraising law issues.

Mr. Hopkins served as chair of the Committee on Exempt Organizations, Tax Section, American Bar Association; chair, Section of Taxation, National Association of College and University Attorneys; and president, Planned Giving Study Group of Greater Washington, DC.

Mr. Hopkins was the series editor of Wiley's Nonprofit Law, Finance, and Management Series. In addition to coauthoring *The Law of Fundraising, Sixth Edition*, he was the author of *The Law of Tax-Exempt Organizations, Twelfth Edition; The Tax Law of Charitable Giving, Sixth Edition; The Tax Law of Private Foundations, Fifth Edition; The Planning Guide for the Law of Tax-Exempt Organizations: Strategies and Commentaries; Bruce R. Hopkins' Nonprofit Law Library* (e-book); *Tax-Exempt Organizations and Constitutional Law: Nonprofit Law as Shaped by the U.S. Supreme Court; Bruce R. Hopkins' Nonprofit Law Dictionary; IRS Audits of Tax-Exempt Organizations: Policies, Practices, and Procedures; The Tax Law of Associations; The Tax Law of Unrelated Business for Nonprofit Organizations; The Nonprofits' Guide to Internet Communications Law; The Law of Intermediate Sanctions: A Guide for Nonprofits; Starting and Managing a Nonprofit Organization: A Legal Guide, Seventh Edition; Nonprofit Law Made Easy; Charitable Giving Law Made Easy; Private Foundation Law Made Easy; 650 Essential Nonprofit Law Questions Answered; The First Legal Answer Book for Fund-Raisers; The Second Legal Answer Book for Fund-Raisers; The Legal Answer Book for Nonprofit Organizations*; and *The Second Legal Answer Book for Nonprofit Organizations*. He is the coauthor, with Thomas K. Hyatt, of *The Law of Tax-Exempt Healthcare Organizations, Fourth Edition*; with David O. Middlebrook, of *Nonprofit Law for Religious Organizations: Essential Questions and Answers*; with Douglas K. Anning, Virginia C. Gross, and Thomas J. Schenkelberg, of *The New Form 990: Law, Policy and Preparation*; with Ms. Gross, of *Nonprofit Governance: Law, Practices, and Trends*; and with Ms. Gross and Mr. Schenkelberg, of *Nonprofit Law for Colleges and Universities: Essential Questions and Answers for Officers, Directors, and Advisors*. He also wrote "Bruce

R. Hopkins' Nonprofit Counsel," a monthly newsletter published by John Wiley & Sons.

Mr. Hopkins received the 2007 Outstanding Nonprofit Lawyer Award (Vanguard Lifetime Achievement Award) from the American Bar Association, Section of Business Law, Committee on Nonprofit Corporations. He was listed in The Best Lawyers in America, Nonprofit Organizations/Charities Law, 2007–2021.

Mr. Hopkins was the Professor from Practice at the University of Kansas School of Law, where he taught courses on the law of tax-exempt organizations.

Mr. Hopkins earned his J.D. and L.L.M. degrees at the George Washington University, his S.J.D. at the University of Kansas, and his B.A. at the University of Michigan. He was a member of the bars of the District of Columbia and the state of Missouri.

Alicia M. Beck is the Philanthropy Director at UMB Bank in Kansas City, Missouri. She is responsible for building long-term client relationships by assisting individual clients, families, and prospects with charitable planning and planned giving options that enable them to have a long-term community as part of their legacy. Prior to UMB, Ms. Beck was an attorney in the law firm of Polsinelli PC, practicing in the firm's Kansas City, Missouri, office. She specializes in advising both nonprofit and for-profit entities. Her clients include national hospital systems, research organizations, private foundations, colleges, universities, associations, social welfare organizations, and governmental entities. Ms. Beck assisted these clients with formation, structure, and operational issues, including fundraising regulation. She also has experience with various tax restructuring issues relating to international entities.

Ms. Beck received her J.D. degree from the University of Kansas School of Law. She received an L.L.M. in taxation from Northwestern University, and a B.A. in Supply and Value Chain Management from Texas Christian University. Ms. Beck is a member of the bars of the states of Illinois, Kansas, and Missouri. She has been involved in the Leukemia & Lymphoma Society and has served on the Board of Directors for the Lyric Opera of Kansas City and Variety, The Children's Charity.

Index